How to Build a Business

in

Seven Simple Steps

By

Wordran Naa Wilson

TABLE OF CONTENTS

MY WHY

My business journey has been inspired by my parents' struggles in business. They had the qualities required to become successes; incredibly hardworking, creative and resilient, and yet they were never enough.

My parents were caught in a continuous cycle of starting a business, the businesses failing, accumulating debt, and experiencing intense frustration before starting a business again to make money.

I spent my childhood watching my parents repeat the same business mistakes and behaviours over and over again; we all felt the pain of another failed venture.

Now, as an adult experienced in business myself, I can see that there were **no barriers**, rather there were **obstacles** for which I now have the solutions.

The book I have written is the book I wish my parents had access to when I was growing up in Ghana, Africa.

It's designed to help you navigate through the murky waters of business, overcome challenges and, most importantly, be in control of your business journey.

AUTHOR'S NOTE

As a small business advisor, the most common question entrepreneurs ask me is; why do their friends and family seem resistant to backing and supporting their business idea? The answers to this is complex, but ultimately, it discourages people from pursuing their business ideas.

The good news is, you have access to resources such as this book, and also, there are many people in the business community who will champion your idea, empower you to overcome obstacles, and help you develop a sustainable business. You may just not have met them yet!

DEDICATION

A huge thank you to:

Mina Wilson

Rudi Lombardo

and Stella Humu Sulaiman.

For your support, love, and encouragement during the book writing process.

HOW THIS BOOK CAN HELP YOU

This book is a manual of valuable information to help you start and run a successful and sustainable business. It's a guide that journeys with you from your initial idea, through business types and models, to finance and marketing. It walks you through the vital steps you need to take in order to start a new business venture.

Statistics show 20% of new businesses fail in their first year, and nearly 50% don't survive to celebrate their fifth birthday. Every business starts at zero, but why do some thrive whilst others fail to survive?

This book and its workbook help you move your business idea forward and show you how to prepare for business success. You are now in the privileged position of being able to avoid many of the common mistakes inexperienced entrepreneurs commonly make at the start of their venture's life!

You are being given information and techniques to improve the chances of business success—the secret is knowing what needs to be done and the appropriate time to do it! After all, if you play a game knowing the rules, you are far more likely to succeed.

Be prepared; it's hard work to build the foundations for a successful business, and you may find that you learn just as much about yourself as you do business.

Business growth goes hand-in-hand with personal growth; Thomas Watson Sr., Chairman, and CEO of International Business Machines said, "To be successful, you have to have your heart in your business, and your business in your heart."

Research shows that writing things down not only helps us to process emotions and information, but also clarify and prioritise goals. These are valuable business skills to develop, and I encourage you to be proactive and complete the recommended exercises in the workbook.

Work steadily through the book and give yourself time to digest the information you are reading so you can apply and refine your responses to suit your unique situation. Be flexible, agile, and open to learning new ways of doing things.

In the words of Peter F. Drucker, Management Consultant, Educator, and Author, "In every success story, you will find someone who has made a courageous decision."

Further, there is little more motivating than seeing the success of people who have taken an entrepreneurial path. My own journey has been heavily influenced by studying their mindsets and achievements. I have applied these observations to my own circumstances.

Hence, I've approached several successful entrepreneurs and asked them key questions about being in business. Their responses are both constructive and inspirational, and you too can benefit from their advice as you go through this book.

So, what are you waiting for? Are you ready to learn how to become a successful entrepreneur?

Don't forget to obtain a copy of the workbook by searching *wordran* in Amazon or scan the code.

CHAPTER I.
INCEPTION / IDEA

WHAT TYPE OF BUSINESS SHOULD I START?

This is the million-dollar question. There are endless possibilities, but not all are equal. It requires you to undertake a degree of soul searching to identify the type of business you should start.

You must connect with your authentic self and be honest about the type of business YOU want—not what your friends/parents/wife/husband, etc. want.

To gain clarity about the direction to take your business, consider the following points:

i.   Choose something you are <u>passionate</u> about.

If you are not interested in the core purpose of the business, you will struggle to maintain the commitment, momentum, and energy to make the venture a success. Besides, you will notice the passion you have for the business is contagious, and this will be recognised by your target audience/customers—which means more sales.

ii.   Choose an industry you have a comprehensive <u>knowledge</u> of.

Starting a new venture can be stressful at the best of times but trying to enter a new industry or learn new skills at the same time can create unnecessary stress. This doesn't mean you should be closed to developing new skills, rather, it is about being realistic about what you can achieve and how you can maintain standards.

iii. Choose a business that will make a profit.

Many new entrepreneurs fail to understand the difference between revenue (total income generated by the business) and profit (the amount the business is left with after all expense deductions). The potential profitability of your business should be explored by undertaking a **break-even analysis** (a financial projection) to evaluate the ease of turning a profit.

WHY A BUSINESS OF YOUR OWN?

When the business idea kicks in, it's easy to suffer from what I call the Hurry Syndrome. You want to get out there, get active, and start creating wealth. However, this is the time to pause, reflect, and ask yourself some key questions.

These key questions help you to gather information and shape your business idea. Now that you have identified the type of business you want to start, it is time to dig deeper and discover your niche within the industry.

This is your opportunity to identify your WHY.

TIP: Your WHY for starting a business MUST provide a solution to a problem somewhere in someone's life or someone's business. *What I call business to audience.* This can be a gap in the market, evolutionary (reinventing the wheel), or revolutionary (something no one has thought of).

By clearly defining your WHY, you will have answers to your HOWs and have good ideas about how to market your business in the future— your customers' pain points will become abundantly clear!

What advice would you give to someone who is at the idea stage of their business?

Find a problem that your product or service will solve. It does not have to be a complicated one; small troubles are often the best. Once you have identified that there is a problem your product or service can solve, you have the ideal opportunity to sell.

Bert Evers
Mentor, Cherie Blair Foundation For Women
Switzerland

Now that you have read this chapter, complete the corresponding exercises in the workbook.

CHAPTER II.
ROADMAP

Before you hand in your resignation letter to focus on your enterprise, it is important to resist the pull of the Hurry Syndrome. You will be familiar with the adage *'fail to prepare and prepare to fail.'*

Statistically, only 44.1% of all businesses celebrate their fifth birthday. Business failure can be attributed to many reasons, but lack of planning is typically the primary cause.

Start as you mean to go on and take control of the situation. Investing time to plan your business is the wisest investment you can make, and it will give you the greatest returns.

How would you motivate someone who is feeling stuck and overwhelmed in their existing business?

Stop! Spend time to reflect where you are now and identify where you would like to be. Plan for the journey ahead—create a roadmap to be in control. Seek professional help or have a step-by-step strategy to help get to your destination. Never give up!

Rudi Lombardo
CEO of Silonplast
Italy

A roadmap is a vital document for success and gives you short and long-term guidance and direction. A roadmap is a powerful tool for your business.

Below are five important steps to create a roadmap for the foundations of a successful and sustainable business.

5 STEPS TO CREATE A ROADMAP FOR STARTUP SUCCESS

1.   Identify a problem in a proven market.

The most prevalent misconception people have about their startup is that it must be revolutionary and unique, but this is rarely the case.

Rather than squandering your time developing a product or service to be **"The Next Big Thing"** focus on ways to solve a problem in an already proven market.

Remember, if it does not currently exist, it is likely the idea will arouse only a limited interest. Identification of a problem in a proven market shows there is already a customer base you can exploit.

2.   Have a vision, mission, and strategy, but overall, be flexible.

How can you achieve success if you don't have defined goals? You need to be clear about what you want to achieve so you can work backward to identify the steps you need to take to achieve them.

Be realistic and set achievable objectives to meet for both the short and long-term. Having a clear vision of what your business will look like in the future will guide you and give direction while you establish and grow the business.

> **What advice would you give to someone who has just started in business?**
>
> *Always be focused on your goal and be confident to grab opportunities, but also give encouragement and support to your employees—their success is your success.*
>
> Martin Larsen
> Managing Director, EP Consult Energies
> Denmark/U.K.

Create a compelling mission statement to articulate the story and ethos behind your business. Often overlooked, a mission statement is a great way to inform decisions and give the business a consistent voice people can relate to.

Undertake a SWOT analysis. A SWOT analysis helps to identify opportunities you can take advantage of and establish where potential risks and challenges may lie. Markets change with fads and trends; a robust SWOT analysis keeps you ahead of the curve so you can react swiftly for a positive outcome.

- **Strengths**
- **Weaknesses**
- **Opportunities**
- **Threats**

A mission statement and business plan help to provide a clear vision, mission, and strategy to guide you through the startup process. They are valuable tools you can use to attract talent and persuade investors.

3. Assemble your A-Team.

A SWOT analysis can highlight skill gaps in the business that need to be addressed. Many new entrepreneurs try to do everything themselves. After all, it feels counter-intuitive to spend money when you are trying to make money; however, this can prove to be a false economy.

Don't be afraid to outsource tasks you don't have the skills to complete to a high standard. Outsourcing allows you to work within a budget and to a set deadline with quality assured, so you can focus on other revenue-creating tasks.

Tasks to consider outsourcing include bookkeeping, web development, digital content, legal work, marketing, and more.

Developing good working relationships with other professionals is key and lessens the burden of making your startup a success. Plus, extending your network of business allies actively helps to promote your business.

4. Build the best product.

Too often, startups seek investment before they have developed the best product for the marketplace. Rather than perfecting their offerings, resources (energy, time, and money) are spent planning and scheduling meetings with investors.

Customers and investors alike will only be attracted to your business if they can see and understand what their money will get them. You need to be able to demonstrate value.

Before you approach investors, your product must be perfected!

5. Develop your niche and generate a buzz.

When starting your business, you'll naturally want to sell as many units of your product as possible. The temptation to market your product or services to as many people as possible is almost irresistible. However, the reality is, not everyone will want your product. With a limited marketing budget, you need every penny spent to attract the people who are most likely to want your product.

Understand the demographics of the customers who will be buying your products or services: the language they use and respond to, where they hang out online, what their pain points are, and what their shared likes and interests are, etc.

Use this information to target consumers by creating quality, informative content—graphs, videos, and blog posts—to share across social media platforms.

Online expert John Rampton says, "Use social media, and develop a content marketing strategy to market your startup. Even if you have an amazing product or service [if] you fail to market it properly, no one will know about it."

Not only will your marketing content provide engaging and valuable information for your target audience, but it will also define you and your startup as industry leaders—a trusted and credible voice of authority.

Now that you have read this chapter, complete the corresponding exercises.

CHAPTER III.
BUSINESS PLAN

A business plan is a formal written document that states the goals of the business, how you intend to achieve them, and the projected timeline for accomplishing them. Typically, a business plan has projections for the first 12 months and annual forecasts for three and five years of trading.

Every startup needs a well-written business plan not only to give you guidance and direction, but also as a tool to attract investors.

The burning question is, how do you write a business plan for your startup business?

The Small Business Administration (SBA) recommends a business plan should include the following:

- o Executive summary
- o Company description
- o Market analysis
- o Organisation and management
- o Service or product
- o Marketing and sales strategy
- o Funding request
- o Financial projections
- o Appendix

Admittedly, this list looks rather intimidating, so I have distilled the information into seven steps you can follow to write a perfect business plan.

How did having a business plan help in starting up your new business HomeDotCare?

As a business owner it has been instrumental in grounding me as to what I set out to achieve which is important as once gets started, it is very easy to get distracted by different options / given conflicting advice. Plus there can be the usual disillusion / despair when business go as planned.

With perseverance, the right packaging, mindset and a solid business plan an entrepreneur has all the necessary tools to make any business a success.

Owusua Ogunbayo
Founder of HomeDotCare,
UK

---

7 STEPS TO WRITE A PERFECT BUSINESS PLAN

Step 1. Research, Research, Research.

Did I mention research? You need to thoroughly research your product, the market, and the objective of your business. There should be no stone left unturned. The good news is that you have the most valuable tool at your disposal; the internet. It is a fantastic source of information to help you gain valuable insights into your potential customers, your competitors, and the market you are entering.

Pay close attention to your competitors; read customer reviews of their business—what they do well, the errors they make, the products they appear to do well with, and the gaps in their offerings.

Read industry-specific websites and keep up to speed with news, forecasts, and trends. Note who the movers and shakers are and who has influence—they will be valuable connections for you to make.

In other words, you need to research the external influencing factors that will affect your business internally.

Step 2. Identify the primary business goal.

You will have several business goals you intend to achieve, however, you must identify the primary goal. By articulating what the primary goal is, you can create an efficient and streamlined roadmap to help you achieve it. The primary goal helps you to define and understand the other 'feeder' goals and objectives that require action to support its attainment.

Investors only finance startups which have their priorities straight. A business plan shows them the routes the business will take to fulfil the goals and ultimately provide them with profit. Make no mistake; their eyes will always be on the profit.

Step 3. Create a company profile.

How can you develop a business that people trust if it is not clearly defined? A company profile is an introduction to your business and informs people (consumers and stakeholders) about the products, services, status, and ethos.

When creating your company profile, write for the audience, rather than yourself. State why you established the business, its history, your vision, the mission statement, and how you have developed the brand. The company profile is your opportunity to make sure the business stands out ahead of the competition—celebrate its unique features!

> **TIP**: If you have a website, your company profile can be adapted for use in the **'About Us'** page.

Step 4. Document all aspects of your business.

Keeping on top of your business' administration is the least appealing aspect of running a company. However, it is important to get into the habit of documenting information from the start.

Develop effective systems and processes for recording information. This will help you manage your business efficiently on a day-to-day basis and also ensure you have access to accurate information as and when you need it—expenses, cash flow, forecasts, and industry projections.

Investors need to see where they will make a return on their money. Having complete business records demonstrates you are professional and have a business with the potential for growth.

TIP: Include seemingly minor details, such as your location strategy and licensing agreements.

Step 5. Have a strategic marketing plan.

A good business plan includes a strategic and aggressive marketing plan. This typically involves detailing marketing goals, such as:

o   Introducing new products

o   Expansion or recovery of existing product markets

o   Entering new areas of business

o   Increasing sales of a specific product, market, or price range

o   Cross-selling (or linking) a product to another

o   Going into long-term contracts with desirable clients

o   Increasing prices without reducing sales figures

o   Refining products

o   Improving product manufacturing/delivery

o   Creating a content marketing strategy

Step 6. Customise to suit the investor.

Business is more than just crunching numbers; it's about developing mutually beneficial relationships. Instinct and first impressions can be the deciding factor for investors, but for the relationship to be a success, you both need to understand what makes the other tick.

Just as every business is unique, every investor is different too. Your business plan's success is reliant on how well it convinces investors to trust your business model. It's a good idea to research the investor to get an understanding of their investing history so you can customise the business plan to suit.

Step 7. Review and modify.

Reviewing and editing is the final stage of writing any piece of content, but it is especially important when it comes to professional documents such as business plans.

You only have one opportunity to make a first impression; therefore, your business plan must be perfect. To gain the support of targeted investors, your plan must be flawless. Check and double-check the correct words or expressions have been used, dates and numbers are accurate, and the document is free from spelling and grammar mistakes.

Failing to amend errors can make you seem unprofessional and indifferent to those you want to impress. Why would anyone invest their hard-earned money in your company if you have made careless errors on such an important document?

Use consistent and professional formatting in the business plan to present it in a logical style, but above all else, ensure the plan is clear, concise, and convincing.

Lastly, review your plan to see if it fits all the steps in this list.

Once done, your business plan is ready!

Now that you have read this chapter, complete the corresponding exercises.

CHAPTER IV.
MARKETING STRATEGIES TO GROW YOUR BUSINESS

S tarting a new business is not easy. You've taken your initial idea, discovered a profitable niche, refined your product, and defined your target audience. It's been hard work, but now the real work starts!

Whether you have products to sell or services to promote, if your target audience doesn't hear about you, the harsh reality is, your business will fail.

Marketing your business is essential—not only to survive but also to thrive and grow. It is critical to adopt dynamic marketing strategies to enhance and develop your brand, make sales, and hit your profit targets.

8 MARKETING STRATEGIES FOR BUSINESS SUCCESS

1. Get to know your customers.

Your customers are the lifeblood of your business. It is important to understand their needs and develop products and services to meet their requirements—so ask them!

Customer feedback provides valuable information to improve your business and product. You may even identify gaps in your offerings that can be exploited for future business growth.

The more you understand your target audience, the greater the opportunity to further the reach of your brand by providing products or services which are relevant to them.

TIP: Gather customer data by including a questionnaire in your checkout process, asking direct questions on your social media accounts, or even by telephoning them. Don't forget to ask for your customers' consent.

---

2. Provide excellent customer service.

No matter how great a product is, the standard of customer service will influence whether you have a repeat customer. Never underestimate how important the customer experience is: *under-promise and over-deliver.*

A happy customer will always recommend your business to their friends and family, but in the same vein, bad news travels fast!

3. Feed existing customers and create room for new opportunities.

Successful businesses don't just have new customers; they have returning customers. It's as important to nurture the relationship with your existing customers as it is to find new prospects. But, be aware: when experiencing a sustained level of success, you should never become complacent and stop looking for new opportunities.

To increase your brand's visibility in the marketplace, regularly publish new content on your website and social media platforms and attend networking events. These activities help to develop and strengthen relationships. Prospects see your business is active and thriving within the industry.

TIP: Send e-mails of upcoming events and promotions, or create a newsletter to update customers of your business' news to retain your business' visibility.

---

4. Use social media.

Social media is a gift to businesses that keeps on giving. Create free accounts on Facebook, Twitter, Instagram, and LinkedIn to increase the visibility of your business online.

Your social media profiles are the easiest way to connect with your target audience in a way they can relate to. However, you must use a consistent, authentic voice, using appropriate language to represent your brand—it must be relevant and relatable to the target audience.

Don't just think social media is all about promoting your brand's message. It also allows you to gain valuable insights and opinions about your business. 'Social listening' provides you with up-to-date information about industry and customer trends and keywords to use in digital marketing.

> **TIP**: If you receive negative comments publicly on your social media profile about the service or products you provided, deal with it professionally and swiftly. Potential customers will see how you are fair, reasonable, and quick to provide a solution—exactly what consumers appreciate. Use the feedback to showcase the strength of your customer services!

5. Attend networking seminars.

As previously mentioned, business is more than number-crunching; it's about building relationships. Networking seminars and meet-ups are a social and effective way to market your business.

People like to know who they are working with; they want more than an online connection and like to have a face to go with the name. If people know you personally, they are more likely to recommend your services in the future.

6. Organise events.

Hosting your own event can be a great way to meet customers and build relationships. Invite some of your existing customers and encourage them to bring their friends.

You may struggle to think about a topic for an event, but you will be surprised about the knowledge you have taken for granted. Your customers and prospects do not have the same level of understanding of your industry and will welcome the opportunity to learn more.

7. Give back to your community.

Developing brand awareness in your local community is another great way of attracting new businesses. Consider sponsoring or participating in a social event to improve your business profile.

TIP: Inform the local media about the social event and publicise it on your social media profiles. Think of this as an opportunity to increase your brand's exposure as much as a goodwill gesture!

8. Measure results and refine your approach as you go.

Every marketing strategy you implement needs to be measurable. This means you need to have some way of tracking how successful the marketing has been.

You have access to website and social media metrics. Track which posts are more popular with visitors—which ones get the most shares, click-throughs, and likes; and those that are less successful.

Some of your marketing efforts will be more effective than others. By tracking and measuring the metrics, you can fine-tune your marketing and focus on the more successful means in the future. Do not be scared to experiment!

TIP: If you are marketing your business through more traditional methods such as flyers or adverts, you can include different codes for each geographical area so you can easily track how and where customers found your business.

Now that you have read this chapter, complete the corresponding exercises.

CHAPTER V.
FINANCING YOUR STARTUP

Thousands of people start businesses each year, and although the types of businesses vary, they share one thing in common—they have had to raise funds to start their venture.

When the economic climate is healthy, it is easier to gain funding from third parties. In times of economic and political uncertainty, the quest is more challenging. However, this does not mean raising funds is not possible; you just have to search a little harder to find it.

To obtain the money you require to set up and start running your business, you have several options.

7 WAYS TO FINANCE YOUR BUSINESS

1. Bank loan

The terms and conditions attached to loans from banks are gradually becoming tougher. If you have a strong credit score, if you have assets, and your taxes are in good shape, you should not have a hard time securing a bank loan.

You must understand fully the terms of the loan and the repayments you will be obligated to honour.

2. Internet loan/peer-to-peer

If you are unable to secure a loan via the traditional banks, there are now many small business online lending options that can loan you up to £500,000. Online applications are easy to complete, and decisions about whether your application is successful are quick—taking anywhere between an hour and a business day, depending on which provider you approach.

As well as internet loans, there are peer-to-peer lenders. money.co.uk is a business loan comparison site for both secured and unsecured loans that could help you grow your business. The significant disadvantage of peer-to-peer loans is that the interest paid is typically higher than comparable traditional loans. However, this is offset by the fact you are dealing directly with the lender and so the criteria are not as strict as traditional bricks-and-mortar banks.

3. Credit cards

Credit cards are an effective and versatile way to finance your small business and extend your cash flow. Credit cards can also provide additional benefits; you can use them to make payments to suppliers, potentially earning discounts, and they often come with supplementary protections and other rewards.

However, to start your business with credit cards, you need to have a healthy credit score to have your application accepted. If you need a credit card for cash advances, you should check the small print for any cash limits and the fees charged for this service.

4. Friends and family

Many entrepreneurs approach friends and family to fund their new business ventures. You have two options: ask them to invest in equity (in effect selling them part of your business) or ask them for a loan.

If you do enter an agreement with your loved ones, it is recommended you formalise the agreement by way of a contract. This will provide them with the assurance you will honour the debt.

You need to ask yourself if you are willing to risk the relationship in the event of the business failing. Always tread carefully when mixing business with family!

5. Angel investors

An angel investor is an individual who provides capital for startups. Ordinarily, they invest in young businesses where most other investors are not prepared to support them.

For startups, angel investors are a welcome source of financing. They typically invest between £10,000 and £2,000,000. Every angel investor has a unique appetite for risk and returns. Some invest independently, and others as part of a syndicate.

To be successful with angel investors, you need to ensure the business plan contains a clear exit strategy for the investor. The exit strategy refers to money for the investors, and not the entrepreneur! Every angel investor will scrutinise the exit strategy to make certain the returns of the investment are maximised for their benefit.

6. Crowdfunding

Some websites, such as Kickstarter and Indiegogo, provide another online opportunity to raise low-interest funds for your new business while having fun at the same time. The more creative and inspiring your crowdfunding pitch is, the more likely you are to hit your target.

This innovative way of financing your business also gives you the opportunity to validate your business idea—failure to achieve the goal suggests there is no thriving market for your idea.

Before choosing a crowdfunding site, read the fine print so you know the size of the cut taken by the platform and what happens at the end if you fail to reach your goal.

7. Sell assets

If you have any valuable assets, such as jewellery or a personal vehicle, this option is perhaps the easiest and safest way to fund a new business.

You won't have to worry about repayments or face any negative consequence, such as damage to your credit score, should the business fail.

> **TIP**: Only sell replaceable assets (i.e., not family heirlooms or items of sentimental value) so you can repurchase an equivalent when you are in better financial shape.

Now that you have read this chapter, complete the corresponding exercises.

CHAPTER VI.
CHOOSING THE BEST LEGAL STRUCTURE FOR YOUR BUSINESS

The legal structure you choose for your new business has far-reaching consequences, and you should not underestimate its importance.

You must spend time assessing the advantages and disadvantages of each structure and choose one that will be effective for you both today and in the future.

Your choice can have a significant impact on the way you do business, and this can have serious consequences, not only on liability and taxes but also on company control.

It is crucial to determine which structure provides the most benefit to your business to help you achieve your organisational and personal financial goals. Below are the common business entities and key factors you need to consider when choosing the appropriate business structure.

WHAT ARE THE DIFFERENT TYPES OF BUSINESS ENTITIES?

1. Sole proprietorship

A sole proprietorship is the simplest and most common form of business entity. In a sole proprietorship, the individual bears both the loss and profits of the business.

If you have decided to be your own boss and start a new business from your house without paying for a physical location, the sole proprietorship is the best option for you. It allows you to be in complete control of the business.

With a sole proprietorship there is no separation or protection between personal and professional property. While this can be a benefit, it could become a problem later as your business grows, and you are responsible for all decisions.

2. Partnership

Unlike a sole proprietorship, a partnership is a form of business owned and controlled by two or more individuals. A partnership is the best option for you if you want to share resources, knowledge, and skills with another person or people. A partnership means profit, loss, and decisions are shared by all parties (depending on the agreement).

3. Limited Liability Company (LLC)

A limited liability company is a hybrid structure that allows owners, partners, or shareholders to limit their liabilities while enjoying the tax benefits and flexibility of a partnership.

Under the LLC, members are protected from personal liability for company debts unless it can be proven they acted unlawfully, unethically, or there is any form of irresponsibility in performing their activities.

The advantage of LLC is that it provides greater protection and separation for companies than businesses owned and controlled by an individual.

4. Corporation

According to law, a corporation is regarded as an entity that is separate from its owners. Unlike other business entities, such as sole proprietorship and partnership, a corporation has its own legal rights independent of the owners—it can sue, be sued, own and sell property and the right of ownership sold in the form of a shares sale.

There are many types of corporations; some common ones are C corporations, S corporations, B corporations, closed corporations, and non-profit corporations.

5. Cooperative

A cooperative business is owned and controlled by the people it serves; its members vote on the mission and direction of the organisation.

Cooperatives vary in size and type but are fundamentally set up to meet defined objectives and are structured to adapt to the members' needs.

KEY FACTORS TO CONSIDER WHEN DECIDING ON A LEGAL STRUCTURE

- Financial needs to start your business
- Personal financial risk
- Scalability – what happens when you grow your business?
- Licenses, permits, and regulations

Depending on your business, the sector, and industry in which it operates, you may need a specific structure to satisfy the legal requirements for licenses, permits, and regulations. (Note: these structure requirements can vary between the local, state, and federal level in the United States.)

You must do your homework and ensure the legal structure you choose is going to be appropriate to obtain the necessary documents— never assume one-size-fits-all!

Once you have registered your business, it can be difficult to change the legal structure. This is another reason why creating a business plan that has detailed timescales is a major benefit—you already know what you want your future business to look like.

Now that you have read this chapter, complete the corresponding exercise.

CHAPTER VII.
PERSONAL DEVELOPMENT

There are most likely thousands of businesses that offer the same products and services your business intends to—YOU are the *exclusive feature* that distinguishes your business from the competition. It's your creativity, drive, resilience, and enthusiasm that will make your business a success.

Starting your own business is a time-consuming, energy-draining experience fraught with extreme highs and lows, but it is also a time when you undergo extreme personal development—sometimes unintentionally.

You must take care of yourself and take responsibility and control of your own journey. Personal development is about self-management: recognising your strengths, skills and qualities; your weaknesses and flaws, and the steps you need to take to maximise your potential.

HOW TO MANAGE YOUR PERSONAL DEVELOPMENT

1. Develop a personal vision.

It's far easier to be motivated and remain in control if you have a purpose and goal to work toward. Reflect on where you want to be next year, in three and five-years' time.

2. Plan your personal development.

Your personal vision needs the equivalent of a business plan to help your dreams become reality. Similarly, plan your personal development with defined goals and realistic, achievable objectives. Your personal development plan will give you direction and highlight the areas where you need to improve.

3. Begin the improvement process.

It's always easier to procrastinate; however, the time to begin a self-improvement program is right now. If you identify an aspect of your personal development plan isn't meeting your expectations or needs, adjust it so it will.

There are many ways to learn and develop; just because one doesn't resonate with you doesn't mean you should give up—resilience is an essential requirement for an entrepreneur.

What would you say to someone who feels like giving up on their business?

Successful businesses never rise overnight—they are not instant. So, when the going gets tough, strive to work within defined strategies, follow the rules and regulations, and keep doing the right things.

Perseverance and focusing on your goals and business' destination is key to not giving up.

Ueta Naoki

CEO Hosoya Marine

Tokyo, Japan

There are many online resources you can access to inspire you. For example, the TED Talks offer a variety of inspirational self-development topics that cover business, science, and tech.

4. Record your personal development.

Journaling is an easy way to record your personal development and keep track of how you are feeling and how you cope and respond to specific situations.

5. Reviewing and revising personal development plans.

Over time, you will collate a useful record of trends in your learning and development. For effective learning, it is essential to review your experiences and reflect on what you have discovered.

Schedule regular reviews of your personal development plan, as your needs will change. This ensures the activities remain relevant to your personal vision as you grow and develop.

Now that you have read this chapter, complete the corresponding exercises.

It's natural to feel overwhelmed starting a new venture. *How to Build a Business in Seven Simple Steps* is a handbook to get you started on the right foot on the start of your entrepreneurial journey.

AFRICAN PROVERB

There's an African proverb that says:

If you want to go fast, go alone; if you want to far, go together.

Hope you've found the book useful on your entrepreneurial journey.

If so, and would like us to go far, then I'd love for you to leave a comment on amazon, share and recommend to others.

All the best and enjoy the journey,

Wordran Naa Wilson.

ACKNOWLEDGEMENTS

A special thanks to those who contributed advice on the topic. Giants who paved the way and set guidelines through example, inspiration through achievement.

Bert Evers, *Mentor, Cherie Blair Foundation For Women,* Switzerland,

Rudi Lombardo, *CEO of Silonplast,* Italy,

Martin Larsen, *Managing Director, EPConsult Energies,* Denmark/U.K.,

Owusua Ogunbayo, *Founder of HomeDotCare*, UK, and

Ueta Naoki, *CEO Hosoya Marine,* Tokyo, Japan.

The QR code will lead you to free business growth resources where you can also read about the author.

Or visit
Business Build Advisory

Printed in Great Britain
by Amazon

57343027R10031